Teaching Strategies for English-Language Learners

- **Teaching Notes**
- **Strategies for Reading, Writing, Speaking and Listening, and Viewing and Representing**
- **Alternative Activities**

HOLT, RINEHART AND WINSTON

A Harcourt Classroom Education Company

Austin · New York · Orlando · Atlanta · San Francisco · Boston · Dallas · Toronto · London

STAFF CREDITS

EDITORIAL

Director
Mescal Evler

Manager of Editorial Operations
Bill Wahlgren

Executive Editor
Kristine E. Marshall

Writing and Editing
Susan Sims Britt, Tressa Sanders,
Jennifer Schwan

Copyediting
Michael Neibergall, *Copyediting
Manager;* Mary Malone, *Senior
Copyeditor;* Joel Bourgeois,
Elizabeth Dickson, Gabrielle
Field, Julie A. Hill, Jane Kominek,
Millicent Ondras, Theresa
Reding, Dennis Scharnberg,
Kathleen Scheiner, *Copyeditors*

Project Administration
Marie Price, *Managing Editor;*
Lori De La Garza, *Editorial
Operations Coordinator;* Thomas
Browne, Heather Cheyne, Mark
Holland, Marcus Johnson,
Jennifer Renteria, Janet Riley,
Kelly Tankersley, *Project
Administration;* Ruth Hooker,
Joie Pickett, Margaret Sanchez,
Word Processing

Editorial Permissions
Janet Harrington, *Permissions
Editor*

ART, DESIGN AND PHOTO

Graphic Services
Kristen Darby, *Manager*

Image Acquisitions
Joe London, *Director;* Tim Taylor,
Photo Research Supervisor; Rick
Benavides, *Assistant Photo
Researcher;* Elaine Tate,
Supervisor; Erin Cone, *Art Buyer*

Cover Design
Sunday Patterson

PRODUCTION
Belinda Barbosa Lopez, *Senior
Production Coordinator*
Simira Davis, *Supervisor*
Nancy Hargis, *Media Production
Supervisor*
Joan Lindsay, *Production
Coordinator*
Beth Prevelige, *Prepress Manager*

MANUFACTURING
Shirley Cantrell, *Supervisor of
Inventory and Manufacturing*

Printed in the United States of America

ISBN 0-03-064743-6
1 2 3 4 5 6 082 04 03 02 01 00

Table of Contents

Table of Contents

To the Teacher

Throughout this guide you will find strategies and activities designed to help English-language learners become active participants in classroom learning communities with their English-speaking peers. Based on current and proven practices for teaching content area subject matter to ELL students, these strategies and activities reflect important ideas about the learner's role and about *language* and *communication,* which are at the heart of *Elements of Language.*

More specifically, the strategies in this guide address the needs of ELL students who are in the early advanced stage of English language acquisition. It is important to note that even though these students may demonstrate oral language proficiency, their proficiency with written language may be behind. The use of intervention strategies begins by identifying where students are having difficulty with language and why, and then guiding them toward strategies that they can use to handle various problems.

GOALS FOR ELL STUDENTS

- To facilitate the development of academic language in order to promote concept acquisition
- To facilitate the development of vocabulary required to learn new concepts
- To facilitate the production of oral and written language to express new concepts

THE ELL STUDENT AND LEARNING NEEDS

Understanding the ELL Student

ELL students probably come from cultures with different traditions and routines. If they were born abroad, ELL students must become familiar with a new environment, a new culture, a new country, a new neighborhood, and a new school. Take into account the following points while working with ELL students in your classroom:

- ELL students may be experiencing culture shock and feel overwhelmed by all of the changes in their environments.
- Many ELL students have experienced deprivation and loss. They may have left people, belongings, and surroundings that were important to their lives. Therefore, they may feel sad or angry about living in a new country.
- ELL students may feel isolated because they do not know English well and do not understand the practices and the traditions in their new environments. They need to feel accepted and encouraged in order to gain confidence and experience a rise in self-esteem.

Detecting ELL Students' Difficulties

Since concept acquisition and development are intricately related to language ability, difficulties related to language acquisition may prevent students from developing new concepts fully. It is important to recognize when ELL students experience such difficulties so that you can help them by reteaching a lesson, reinforcing a learning activity, or clarifying an idea previously presented. Below are some of the classroom behaviors that may be indicative of the difficulties related to the development of academic language.

Behaviors That Indicate Problems	
Behavior	**Example**
Lack of participation	The student may put his or her head down or refuse to answer a question.
Incorrect responses	The student continually gives incorrect responses even when questions have been simplified or additional prompts have been provided.
Mixing native language and English	The student speaks or writes in both English and his or her native language because a concept is not completely understood.
Over or under extension of concepts	The student fails to recognize examples of a concept (under) or includes examples that are not part of the concept (over).
Misunder- standing	The student may not be able to answer questions or follow directions because he or she does not understand what is being asked.
Difficulty in literal or inferential reading com- prehension	The student may not be familiar with the words in the text or the ideas that the words represent. The student may not have prior knowledge of a concept.
Native language interference	The student may inappropriately generalize native language elements onto English. For example, Spanish-speaking students may omit the verbs *do, does,* and *did* in interrogative phrases or sentences since in Spanish they are not used.

To the Teacher (continued)

Behaviors That Indicate Problems (continued)	
Behavior	**Example**
Cultural miscues	The student may not have prior knowledge or personal experiences from which to draw a correct response.
Inappropriate rhythm, tone, and inflection	The student may not be familiar with the words or punctuation within a text.
Uneasiness in using idioms and expressions	The student may translate an idiom word-for-word. Therefore, the student may be confused by the meaning.

GENERAL STRATEGIES FOR INSTRUCTING ELL STUDENTS

By recognizing ELL students' personal situations and identifying their difficulties, you can address their learning needs better. Following are general strategies you can use to motivate ELL students and to support their learning.

- Recognize that the level of literacy achievement in the students' native languages may be obscured by a lack of facility with the English language.
- Note that ELL students may show more ability to express themselves in a social situation than in a learning situation. Social and academic English vary considerably, so classroom practices should take this into account.
- Recognize that it takes time to learn concepts in a familiar language, let alone a new one. ELL students need time to show their proficiency in English.
- Recognize that ELL students' prior knowledge bases were not developed around the cultural traditions of English. They will need help in developing strategies to activate their own prior knowledge, which is important to constructing meaning.
- Draw analogies to past experiences and provide opportunities for students to share their own experiences. This will help ELL students activate their prior knowledge.
- Help ELL students deal with culturally unfamiliar topics by doing what you do when you introduce a new topic to the entire class: Place it in a familiar context. Bring the topic to life and encourage students to draw upon their personal experiences and knowledge.
- Use role-playing, objects, pictures, and graphic organizers to create associations and support meaning. Use gestures and facial expressions to cue feelings and moods.

To the Teacher *(continued)*

STRATEGIES TO FACILITATE LANGUAGE DEVELOPMENT

- Paraphrase questions. By restating questions, you can reinforce ELL students' existing knowledge and encourage the acquisition of new language.
- Ask questions and encourage ELL students to offer explanations and summaries. This allows you to determine if students understand new material.
- To simplify a question, try replacing lengthy or complex sentences with shorter, declarative phrases or sentences.
- Pair ELL students with proficient native English speakers. Heterogeneous grouping allows the modeling of English—both social and academic—to occur in a natural context. Cooperative-learning situations also help all students recognize the value of cultural and ethnic diversity.

The following are strategies and activities that can be used for all ELL students or for those students who require additional support in vocabulary and concept development, reading, writing, and understanding and producing oral language. When using any of these strategies, explain and model the strategies to students so that they can integrate these as part of their own learning strategies. The activities can be adapted to any unit or topic.

Vocabulary Development/Concept Development

You can facilitate the acquisition of new vocabulary and new concepts by using activities or materials that provide a context familiar to the students.

Use context-rich activities. Demonstrate the use of new vocabulary in situations related to ELL students' experiences. Where appropriate, use the context provided by concepts or literature the students have already learned. The use of the classroom, the school, and the students' environment to build, develop, and exemplify new vocabulary and concepts provides context in the present, which makes the activity more concrete to the student.

Control the content. When teaching new vocabulary, present words and phrases embedded in sentences or text well known to ELL students. Each sentence or portion of text should focus on only one new word or phrase. This allows the students to concentrate on the acquisition of the target language without having to be concerned with new vocabulary and new concepts at the same time.

To the Teacher *(continued)*

Control the vocabulary. When introducing and developing new concepts, control the complexity of the language. Learning new concepts and new vocabulary at the same time is loaded with too many unknowns and tends to impede the acquisition of new material. Therefore, use language that does not present difficulties so that the focus is on the new concept.

Reading Comprehension

The greatest challenge in the acquisition of new academic language and new concepts is to make text comprehensible to students so that concept development can proceed logically.

Group text in small units. Break long text into smaller units such as paragraphs. Well-constructed paragraphs usually have one main idea with supporting details, so they can stand alone without losing meaning. Use these units to identify the students' difficulties and teach to those areas. After working with the target paragraphs, reconstruct the whole text and restate the active-reading questions or the goal of the reading.

Identify main ideas. Identify the main idea in the text as well as the supporting details. Explain to ELL students how the details support the main idea.

Paraphrase and rephrase text. Simplify text by paraphrasing and rephrasing sections of text, such as sentences or short paragraphs, using language familiar to ELL students. Break down complex sentences into simple sentences. Help clarify the intention and meaning of each sentence, and reconstruct the original sentence afterward.

Writing

You can help ELL students become more proficient with written language by using activities that simplify the writing process.

Guide the writing. With ELL students, brainstorm vocabulary related to a topic. As students brainstorm, you or a scribe can write the words and phrases on chart paper or on the chalkboard. Have students review the list of words and phrases, and encourage them to use the vocabulary orally to describe, explain, or illustrate the target topic. Then, have each student write on the chalkboard a sentence that relates to the topic. With the group, organize the sentences into one or two paragraphs. Correct the grammatical errors and explain them to students. Finally, have the students read the final product.

To the Teacher *(continued)*

You can also help ELL students to improve the writing by suggesting alternative language, more supporting details, or additional facts.

Use peer review. Native speakers of English can help ELL students throughout the writing process. For example, native speakers of English can review the organization of written assignments and make suggestions so that the ELL students' ideas are clearly communicated. Native speakers can help ELL students with elaboration by pointing out areas where ELL students may need to add details to create a complete picture. Native speakers of English can also be useful in locating and correcting problems with grammar, usage, and mechanics in the ELL students' papers.

Modify writing assignments. To help ELL students develop an idea, consider having them develop a topic in a shorter writing assignment. For instance, an ELL student writing a persuasive piece could state his or her opinion, fully elaborate on one reason, and provide a call to action in one paragraph. ELL students may also benefit from developing shorter writing products so that they can concentrate on word choice, grammar, and punctuation.

Listening

Multiple opportunities for listening, with different goals, enhance the development of language comprehension.

Promote active, focused listening. Provide different goals for listening. For example, ask ELL students to listen for specific vocabulary related to a concept during an oral discussion. Then, have students write on a piece of paper the target words and the phrases or sentences in which the target words are embedded. Students can add to this list as you continue the discussion.

Use checklists. Provide lists of words and have ELL students check the ones they hear during a discussion or an oral reading activity. This strategy will reinforce the words that are necessary in understanding a concept.

Use text. Provide ELL students with a hard copy of the text to which they are listening. Have them focus on different elements of diction, such as emphasis, rhythm, and accentuation. For example, students can highlight words that they notice are emphasized during a reading.

To the Teacher *(continued)*

Ask questions. Provide questions to ELL students that will need to be answered after listening to a discussion, an oral reading activity, or an audiotape. This allows you to check their understanding of what they have heard.

Speaking

ELL students should be encouraged to practice their linguistic skills in academic arenas. Oral activities in which ELL students are prompted to voice their opinions or share personal experiences help them build confidence in their speaking abilities.

Ensure comprehension. When ELL students have difficulties in presenting oral materials, ensure comprehension of the material by clarifying, reviewing, and discussing the concepts and the vocabulary.

Model and tape the presentation. Provide ELL students with a taped model presentation of their material (you or a proficient English-speaking student can record it). Help students analyze the patterns and rhythms of the language, and encourage several listening sessions. Have students practice their oral presentations with a group of peers.

Student Self-Monitoring

By monitoring their own learning, ELL students are able to recognize the strategies that work best for them when they encounter difficulties. Consider the following activities to help students monitor their learning:

- Encourage ELL students to check their comprehension when reading or listening. To do this, students can summarize information or answer questions.
- Ask ELL students to identify the difficulties they encounter when learning new lessons and the strategies that work for them. Then, assist students in developing a plan that includes specific strategies, which will help them achieve learning. Finally, have students evaluate their plans by discussing how their plans worked and what changes they may need to make in the future.

By providing ELL students with different activities and strategies, you can help them achieve the goals of developing academic language, acquiring vocabulary to learn new concepts, and producing oral and written language. More importantly, though, you are providing a nonthreatening environment in which ELL students become more self-confident and capable of many levels of communication.

Chapter Objectives:
- To identify the stages of the reading process
- To identify the stages of the writing process
- To identify the connections between reading and writing

Key Concepts for English-Language Learners:
ELL students often require additional support and practice in order to understand key ideas expressed in English. As you work through this introductory chapter, emphasize the following key concepts: *reading process, writing process, prewriting, draft, revising,* and *publishing.*

Introducing the Chapter (pages 2–3)

Building Background
To become good readers, English-language learners need to understand the connection between strategy and comprehension. Many ELL students approach reading as a process in which the reader focuses on unfamiliar vocabulary words. When ELL students focus on the meanings of words, they often overlook the main ideas in the text.

Writing is viewed by many ELL students as submitting a product to the teacher for correction. They may put their focus on grammar and punctuation while neglecting organization and clarity. It will help ELL students if you emphasize that their writing will be assessed on the basis of content and organization.

Relating to Personal Experiences/Making Cultural Connections
Reading and writing skills may be taught differently in different cultures. Explain to ELL students that this introduction will help them understand how this textbook will teach reading and writing skills. One of the main focuses of *Elements of Language* is that reading and writing are both processes. Explore this focus by writing *process* on the board. Then, create a cluster diagram by having students share ideas they relate to the word *process.* Finally, ask students to predict what they will learn about the reading and writing processes as they read the introduction.

READING AS A PROCESS: | (pages 4–8)

Building Background

Before you begin this section, explain to students the following points:

- All good readers use strategies. Expert readers use them automatically and unconsciously.
- When learning to read in a second language, most readers need to relearn the strategies they had come to use automatically in their native languages.
- Learning to use reading strategies requires frequent practice.
- Reading strategies help the reader understand the main ideas in the text, even when some of the language is unclear.

PREREADING (PAGE 5) As you review each prereading strategy, ask students to provide an example of when they may have used the strategy in their own reading. You might also want to model one or two strategies. For example, you could provide a reading selection that has headings, graphics, or boldfaced items to show how to preview a text in order to make predictions.

WHILE READING (PAGES 6–7) After you have reviewed the strategies on pages 6–7, have students review the red annotations on page 7 to identify the strategies a reader used while reading the accompanying selection. Ask students to suggest other annotations that would illustrate additional strategies a reader could use.

AFTER READING (PAGE 8) You may wish to explain to ELL students that post-reading strategies help readers recognize when they have not understood the text and need to seek clarification. Post-reading strategies also help readers connect what they have read to other texts and experiences.

WRITING AS A PROCESS: | (pages 9–14)

Building Background

Before discussing the chart on page 9, have ELL students work with a partner to predict the stages of the writing process. Tell students to think about the steps they take to complete a writing assignment. Then, have the pairs compare their predictions with the chart.

PREWRITING (PAGE 10) Explain to ELL students that during the prewriting stage writers plan what they are going to write about and how they are going to organize their ideas. Stress the importance of being prepared and discuss how the strategies on page 10 will help students prepare to write.

WRITING (PAGE 11) As you discuss the strategies on page 11, explain how writers follow the plans they prepared during the prewriting stage. However, emphasize that writers can rewrite their thesis statements, gather more information, or change the organization of their papers in this stage as well.

REVISING (PAGE 12) Point out that the revision stage focuses on looking at the content, organization, and style of the draft. Therefore, writers should concentrate on what they say and how they say it before they consider the correctness of their writing.

PUBLISHING (PAGES 13–14) During the publishing stage writers should focus on the correctness of their writing. Remind ELL students that correcting errors in grammar, usage, and mechanics helps the writer's intended audience to understand the writer's ideas clearly.

CHART: THE READING-WRITING CONNECTION (PAGE 14) Review the chart on page 14 to be sure ELL students grasp the relationship between reading and writing. You might have students choose a bullet point from the *Reading Process* column and the *Writing Process* column and explain how he or she plans to use these strategies in the future.

CHOICES: (page 15)

Relating to Personal Experiences

LITERATURE: 4. APPROACHING DIFFERENT TEXTS (PAGE 15) Modify this activity to allow ELL students to read passages written in their native languages. Students may want to choose authors, poets, magazines, and books that are familiar to them. Reading texts in their native languages will also help students' comprehension, allowing them to focus on the reading strategies.

Reflecting on Experiences

Chapter Objectives:
- To read a personal reflection
- To write a personal reflection
- To make a video reflection

Key Concepts for English-Language Learners:
ELL students often require frequent repetition, in a variety of contexts, in order to understand key ideas in academic discourse. As you work through the chapter, use the following key concepts frequently: *personal reflection, narrative details, descriptive details,* and *inferences.*

PREVIEW:

Introducing the Chapter (pages 16–17)

Relating to Personal Experiences
Although ELL students may have a working knowledge of the concept *personal reflection,* language constraints may prevent them from active class participation. Engage ELL students in a discussion to help them use and enrich relevant vocabulary. Use the following prompts to begin the discussion:

- Tell about a time when learning about another person's experiences and feelings affected you or changed you in some way.
- Tell about a funny experience you have had, or how you met a person who has made a difference in your life.
- What are some different ways that people express their thoughts and feelings about their experiences?

On the board list details ELL students supply that develop the concept of *personal reflection.* Ask ELL students to identify any words that are new to them; go over those words. Keep a running list of the new words on the board, and add to the list as words are introduced during the lesson.

Building Background
Ask ELL students to create drawings or use magazine images to create collages that represent important events in their lives. This may help ELL students with limited vocabularies communicate relatively complex ideas. Break the entire class into small groups, which include native English speakers, and have ELL students present their drawings or collages. Make sure ELL students are prepared to respond to questions such as the following:

- What does the drawing/collage represent and why is it important?

- Does the drawing represent something you have learned about yourself or others?
- What is the most important thing you would like other people to understand about your drawing?

After the presentations, ask students what generalizations they can make about expressing personal thoughts and feelings. What can they learn from the personal reflections of other people? List responses on the board, and reserve them for building background during the Reading and Writing Workshops. This activity helps ELL students explore and expand vocabulary that applies to personal reflection.

Making Cultural Connections

In some cultures, personal reflection may be expressed primarily through an oral tradition. For example, many families have stories that are handed down from one generation to another describing experiences of emigration, immigration, and assimilation. Encourage ELL students to share these stories with the class. Through this activity, ELL students can develop and enrich oral language skills while celebrating their heritages; native English speakers have an opportunity to expand perspectives.

READING WORKSHOP:

Reading a Personal Reflection (pages 18–27)

Building Background/Making Cultural Connections

Since writing about relatively mundane experiences may not be as prevalent in many societies and cultures as it is in the United States, some students may have difficulty understanding why Annie Dillard would write publicly about her empathy for an insect. To prepare ELL students for Annie Dillard's personal reflection, develop a brief discussion using one of the following approaches:

- Guide ELL students to understand what personal reflections are, who writes them, what their purposes are, and where they are found. You may wish to use some examples from books and magazines such as *Reader's Digest* and *National Geographic*. You might also ask students to locate some other examples on their own.
- Guide ELL students to recognize how a seemingly small event, such as losing a favorite object or observing a scrap of paper sail with the breeze, can have lasting effects on someone's life. Encourage students to make a connection with the chapter preview activities; call their attention to the generalizations they made about expressing personal thoughts and feelings and what they thought could be learned from the personal reflections of other people.

Working with Academic Language/Building Vocabulary

PREPARING TO READ (PAGE 18) Before ELL students read the excerpt from *An American Childhood*, be sure that they understand the terms *inference, narrative details,* and *descriptive details,* which are introduced on page 18. Make a two-column chart on the board. Label the headings *narrative details* and *descriptive details.* Present a captioned action photo from a magazine or newspaper, or use the illustration on page 16. Have students discuss what they think is happening. List details under *narrative details* on the chart. Then, ask students to describe what they see, using as many adjectives as possible. List responses under *descriptive details.* Encourage students to use the information they've gathered to make an educated guess about how the photographer wanted viewers to feel about the subject. List responses on a separate area of the board. When students have finished responding, label the list *inferences.*

READING THE SELECTION (PAGES 19–20) Before reading the selection, present unfamiliar vocabulary to students. Be sure students understand the meanings of the following terms used in the personal reflection on pages 19–20: *searing, crippled, emerged, crumpled, deformed,* and *vigor.*

To provide ELL students with a strategy for figuring out unfamiliar words, you may wish to present the Vocabulary Mini-Lesson, "Using Multiple-Meaning Words," on page 26.

To guide students through reading the personal reflection, select from the general strategies provided at the beginning of this booklet. In addition, you may wish to modify the active-reading questions embedded in the selection, for example:

- What did the Polyphemus moth look like? (question 2, page 19)
- How do you think the author feels about Shadyside? What makes you think so? (question 3, page 20)
- What do you think will happen to the moth? Explain. (question 4, page 20)

Another way to approach the active-reading questions is to provide alternative questions for students to discuss, for example:

- At what time in the author's life did she witness the emergence of the moth from its cocoon?
- How does the author let you know that this event was important to her?

You may also wish to modify "First Thoughts on Your Reading" on page 21 in this way:

- Why do you think the writer repeats the information that the mason jar is too small? (question 1)
- How do you think the writer wants you to feel about the moth? (question 2)

READING SKILL: MAKING INFERENCES (PAGES 21–23) ELL students are more likely to develop a practical understanding if you work with them first on the "Reading Focus: Narrative and Descriptive Details" on pages 24–25. This enables them to access information in the text that is relevant to making an inference. Tips for working with ELL students follow:

- The process of making inferences and generalizations is bound to personal experiences within one's culture. You might engage the whole class in the "Cooperative Learning: Discussing the Effects of Culture" on page 21 in the Annotated Teacher's Edition.
- Guide ELL students to make inferences about Annie Dillard's experience. For example, read aloud the first paragraph of the selection on page 19. Ask: When do you think this personal reflection was written? What clues tell you this? Help ELL students recognize that to make these inferences they connect their own knowledge and common sense to information in the text.

READING FOCUS: NARRATIVE AND DESCRIPTIVE DETAILS (PAGES 24–25) In this section, ELL students will require assistance with the concepts *narrative details, descriptive details, dialogue, similes, metaphors,* and *personification.*

- Draw a web on the board to help students connect the concept of *narrative details* with the *Who? What? When?* and *Where?* questions. Then, invite students to locate examples of each in the reading selection.
- Tell students that descriptive details help readers picture in their minds what is happening and where it is happening. Explain that sights, sounds, smells, and imaginative comparisons are examples of descriptive details. Ask students to find specific examples in the selection and add the examples to the web.

Reflecting on Experiences *(continued)*

WRITING WORKSHOP:

Writing a Personal Reflection (pages 28–49)

Building Background/Relating to Personal Experiences

PREWRITING (PAGES 28–37) ELL students may have greater facility speaking in English than writing in English. Consider the following modifications to help students develop a personal reflection essay:

- Suggest that students write about experiences which they have already recounted to someone.
- ELL students may feel intimidated having to attend to tone and voice in written English. Suggest that they tape-record their experiences before they start writing. Brainstorming orally enables ELL students to use their rich speaking vocabularies to express their true feelings and attitudes. Taping might also help students develop their English writing voices while they continue to attend to other issues in composition.
- Remind ELL students to take cultural differences into account as they write for a wider audience. ELL students may need to explain details such as customs or traditions from their cultures.
- Use graphic organizers to help ELL students select and organize important ideas and details for their essays: background information, events, people and places, dialogue, and thoughts and feelings about the events. The graphic organizer on pages 33–34 might be appropriate.

Working with Text Structures

WRITING (PAGES 38–41) Consider the following approaches to help ELL students have a satisfying writing experience:

- Since ELL students are still acquiring writing proficiency in English, you might have them develop a shorter composition.
- Review the Framework for a personal reflection on page 38; help students locate the parts of the Framework in A Writer's Model on pages 39–40 and in A Student's Model on page 41.

REVISING (PAGES 42–45) Pair ELL students with students who are proficient or native English speakers to make revisions. ELL students might find it helpful to work with a modified set of Content and Organization Guidelines on page 42. Although you may have ELL students focus on questions 2, 3, and 5, ask students to check whether they have provided adequate background information. Make sure that the significance of the experience is stated in the last paragraph.

Working with Sentence Structures

SECOND READING: STYLE (PAGES 43–45) Students whose native language sentence structure is naturally long may have difficulty breaking up sentences rather than combining short, choppy ones. Use sentences from students' essays and work with the group to develop models for varying sentence lengths. Then, have partners work together and choose two or three sentences in their articles to revise according to the models.

Working with Grammar

SUBJECT-VERB AGREEMENT (PAGE 46) Some students may be confused by seeing that third-person singular verbs end in –s and plural nouns also end in –s. Explain that an –s on the end of a word does not always indicate that the word is plural. Remind students that *agreement* means a singular subject takes a singular verb and a plural subject takes a plural form of the verb. Guide students through the examples and practice items in the Grammar Link on page 46, and have students work with native speakers to locate any problems with this form of agreement in their papers.

FOCUS ON VIEWING AND REPRESENTING:

Making a Video Reflection (pages 50–52)

Building Viewing and Representing Skills

To help ELL students with this part of the chapter, use the following activities and approaches:

- Not all ELL students are familiar with video techniques and terminology. To assess students' level of understanding and provide the necessary support, invite students to pantomime the transitions listed on page 51: cut, dissolve, fade-in, fade-out, close-up, and wipe. Clarify as needed.
- If they are filming their video reflections, ELL students may feel more comfortable using voice-overs than direct taping of dialogue. Give them ample opportunity to practice and perfect their voice-overs. Assure students that they can retape if they are not satisfied with their performances.
- If ELL students are presenting still photographs or drawings rather than a video, they may feel more comfortable presenting to small groups rather than to the entire class.

CHOICES:

(page 53)

Building Viewing and Representing Skills

VIEWING AND REPRESENTING: 4. THE LAND THAT TIME FORGOT (PAGE 53) ELL students may especially enjoy this activity. Extend the activity by having pairs of students exchange illustrations to see if they can interpret the messages.

Exploring Comparisons and Contrasts

Chapter Objectives:
- To read a comparison-contrast article
- To write a comparison-contrast essay
- To compare and contrast media coverage

Key Concepts for English-Language Learners:
Use the following key concepts frequently, and in a variety of contexts, to support ELL students' understanding in academic discourse: *compare, contrast, main idea, supporting details, thesis, block method,* and *point-by-point method.*

PREVIEW: ## Introducing the Chapter (pages 54–55)

Building Background/Relating to Personal Experiences
Provide opportunities for ELL students to compare and contrast things they know. Use one of the following prompts:

- Tell a partner about a time when you chose a movie. What did you think about in order to make your choice? How were the movies you considered alike or similar? How were they different?
- What are some of the choices you have made today? Explain the process you completed to make a decision.

Making Cultural Connections
Invite ELL students to compare and contrast aspects of their home cultures with aspects of the culture in the United States. Use categories such as clothing styles, music, recreation, or food. Group ELL students with native English speakers. Have each group record similarities and differences. Allow time for the groups to discuss their results.

READING WORKSHOP: ## Reading a Comparison-Contrast Article (pages 56–65)

Working with Academic Language/Building Vocabulary
PREPARING TO READ (PAGE 56) Before you present the article on pages 57–59, be sure that ELL students understand the terms *main idea, supporting details, block method,* and *point-by-point method,* which are introduced on page 56.

Students may not be familiar with the two comparison-contrast structures. Put the following outlines on the board:

Exploring Comparisons and Contrasts *(cont'd)* PAGES 54-89

Block Method	Point-by-Point Method
A. Subject I	**A.** Point 1
1. Point 1	**1.** Subject I
2. Point 2	**2.** Subject II
3. Point 3	
	B. Point 2
B. Subject II	**1.** Subject I
1. Point 1	**2.** Subject II
2. Point 2	
3. Point 3	**C.** Point 3
	1. Subject I
	2. Subject II

Guide ELL students to complete the two outlines using this information: Subject I: Summer, Subject II: Winter; Point 1: Weather, Point 2: Clothing, Point 3: Sports. If ELL students understand the organization possibilities of comparison-contrast essays, they will be able to check their understanding as they read.

READING THE SELECTION (PAGES 57–59) Before reading the selection, present unfamiliar vocabulary from pages 57–59. Be sure ELL students understand the meanings of the following terms or phrases: *stemming from, conundrum, cardinal, gyratory, dead ends, roundabout, spin-offs, U-turn, "rules of thumb," gross, orient, pentagonal, abutting, patronymic, appendages, perusal, emblazoned, dashboard, founder,* and *incompatibility.*

To provide ELL students with a strategy for figuring out the meanings of unfamiliar words in a comparison-contrast article, you may wish to present the Vocabulary Mini-lesson, "Comparison-Contrast Context Clues," on page 64. Remind ELL students to use this strategy as they read the selection as well as the instructional text in the chapter.

You may also wish to modify the active-reading questions embedded in the selection as follows:

- Driving in Britain is different than driving here. What differences does this paragraph point out? The paragraph heading is a clue. (question 2, page 57)
- How do you think American road names are different from British road names? (question 5, page 58)
- How are the subheads helpful to a reader? (question 6, page 59)

Exploring Comparisons and Contrasts *(cont'd)* PAGES 54-89

Clarify the term *implies* that appears in "First Thoughts on Your Reading," question 3 on page 60. Explain that *to imply* means "to state or show something indirectly."

READING SKILL: MAIN IDEA AND SUPPORTING DETAILS (PAGES 60–62) In this section, ELL students will require assistance with the concept *implied main idea.* First, choose a short paragraph that contains a stated main idea. Have students identify the main idea and the supporting details. Then, introduce a paragraph that has an implied main idea. Show students how the supporting details can be examined in order to determine the main idea.

READING FOCUS: COMPARISON-CONTRAST STRUCTURE (PAGES 62–63) Tell ELL students that they can look at the subheads to determine which organizational method the writer used in the reading selection. Point out that the subheads name a different point, which is then developed about both countries. Therefore, the writer uses the point-by-point method.

Using the subheadings, students can begin to organize the information in a graphic organizer. Tell students to copy either the green graphic organizer on page 63 or the point-by-point outline you wrote on the board earlier.

WRITING WORKSHOP:

Writing a Comparison-Contrast Essay (pages 66–85)

Building Background/Relating to Personal Experiences
PREWRITING PAGES (66–73) Consider these modifications to help students as they develop their comparison-contrast essays:

- Guide ELL students toward topics that relate to their experiences. For example, students may want to compare an aspect of their home cultures to one from the culture of the United States.
- Encourage students who are acquiring a writing vocabulary to focus on a single, well-defined audience. This focus will help students match their purpose of writing a comparison-contrast essay to their audience.
- As ELL students gather information, have them work with partners to determine what is relevant to their topic. Partners, acting as potential readers, can place a check mark next to facts that are relevant.
- Have ELL students use graphic organizers to record key aspects of their papers. The graphic organizers on pages 72–73 might be especially appropriate for students to use.

Exploring Comparisons and Contrasts *(cont'd)* PAGES 54-89

Working with Text Structures

WRITING (PAGES 74–77) You can use the following approaches to help ELL students have a satisfying experience writing their comparison-contrast essays:

- ELL students may not be familiar with the structure or component parts of a typical comparison-contrast essay. Review the Framework for a comparison-contrast essay on page 74, and show students how the parts mentioned in the Framework appear in A Writer's Model on pages 75–76 and A Student's Model on page 77. You may wish to provide some other brief examples of comparison-contrast writing using student samples you have collected. Have students identify the structure of these additional models.
- Since ELL students are still acquiring writing proficiency in English, you might have them develop a shorter composition. Consider having them develop a comparison-contrast paragraph that discusses one point of comparison.

REVISING (PAGES 78–81) ELL students may find it helpful to concentrate on two or three items in the Content and Organization Guidelines on page 78. Questions 2, 3, and 4 focus on the essential elements of an effective comparison-contrast piece.

Building Vocabulary

SECOND READING: STYLE (PAGES 79–81) While it may be natural for native English speakers to use adverbs as they make comparisons, many ELL students will need guided practice using adverbs to emphasize important points. Review with students the examples and practice items that appear on pages 422–425.

Working with Grammar

USING COMPARATIVE AND SUPERLATIVE FORMS (PAGE 82) English-speakers are accustomed to signaling comparison or contrast by using *more, most, less,* or *least* before a modifier, or by adding *–er* or *–est* to the end of a modifier. However, the linguistic rules differ in other languages. Spanish, for example, does not use suffixes to form comparatives and superlatives. Remind ELL students to avoid double comparisons. Review the examples and practice items in the Grammar Link on page 82 and have students work with proficient English speakers to locate any problems with comparative and superlative forms in their essays. Refer students who need additional practice to pages 620–625.

Exploring Comparisons and Contrasts *(cont'd)* PAGES 54-89

FOCUS ON VIEWING AND REPRESENTING:

Comparing and Contrasting Media Coverage (pages 86–88)

Building Viewing and Representing Skills

The following approaches can help ELL students compare and contrast media:

- Have students work in small groups and begin by discussing which news story to select. Encourage ELL students to ask their group members questions for clarification.
- Have each student in a group focus on one element. For example, they might examine attention-getting elements, visual images, and sources.
- Present the answers to the questions in Your Turn 10 on page 88 orally as a group.

You may also want to refer students to pages 928–938 in the Quick Reference Handbook for more information about the media.

CHOICES:

(page 89)

Making Cultural Connections

LITERATURE 2. MOVIE *VS.* BOOK (PAGE 89) Suggest that ELL students choose a movie and a book from their native cultures to compare and contrast. Encourage them to present these works to the class and draw comparisons between their native cultures and American culture as a whole, wherever possible.

Examining Causes and Effects

Chapter Objectives:
- To read a cause-and-effect article
- To write a cause-and-effect explanation
- To analyze the effects of TV

Key Concepts for English-Language Learners:
Use the following key concepts frequently, and in a variety of contexts, to support ELL students' understanding of important ideas: *cause, effect, inference, causal chains,* and *logical progression.*

PREVIEW:

Introducing the Chapter (pages 90–91)

Relating to Personal Experiences/Building Background

1. To introduce the chapter, provide opportunities for ELL students to share their own experiences with cause and effect. Use one of the following prompts to explore the concept of cause and effect:

   - Tell about a current event—something you read in the newspaper or heard on a newscast. What happened? Why did it happen? How did it turn out?
   - Think about a natural event, such as thunder, a sunset, or the rain. When you were a small child, what did you think caused this event?
   - When you hear the words *cause* and *effect*, what do you think of?

2. Jot these sentence frames on the board side by side: *I finished my work early so _____. I arrived late because _____.* Have students take turns completing the sentences. Write responses on the board under the appropriate frame. Invite students to identify the causes and the effects in the statements. You might also ask ELL students to provide examples of cause-effect statements in their first languages.

Making Cultural Connections
Many cultures have myths or folktales that explain natural events, such as why it rains or what causes thunder. Invite ELL students to share myths or folktales of this type from their native cultures. Have students share their insights about why myths and folktales start and why they are carried from one generation to another.

Examining Causes and Effects *(continued)*

READING WORKSHOP:

Reading a Cause-and-Effect Article (pages 92–103)

Building Background

Some ELL students may not be familiar with Yellowstone National Park and its history as a protected open and recreational space of natural beauty. Consider the following activities to prepare students to read the article:

- Display a map and show students the location of Yellowstone National Park.
- Invite anyone in the class who has been to a national park anywhere in the world to share some experiences.
- Invite ELL students to talk about parks and other protected areas in their native countries.

Working with Academic Language/Building Vocabulary

PREPARING TO READ (PAGE 92) Before you present the selection on pages 93–94, be sure students understand the terms *inference, causes, effects,* and *causal chains,* which are introduced on page 92. Make a connection to students' activities in the "Introducing the Chapter" section. For example, to explain the concept *inference,* call students' attention to the sentences they created using the frames. Use the discussion on myths and folktales to illustrate *causal chains.*

READING THE SELECTION (PAGES 93–94) Before reading the selection, present unfamiliar vocabulary to students. Be sure they understand the meanings of the following terms used in the article on pages 93–94: *magnificent, biodiversity, amassed, retardant-dropping, therapeutic, scorched, rejuvenated,* and *abundance.* Keep the words on the board for reference during the lesson. Add any other selection words that might present difficulty.

To provide ELL students with a strategy for figuring out the meanings of unfamiliar words, you may also want to present the Vocabulary Mini-Lesson, "Suffixes," on page 102. Remind ELL students to use this strategy as they read the selection as well as the instructional text in the chapter.

To guide students through the article, select from the general strategies for vocabulary and comprehension provided at the beginning of this booklet. In addition, you may want to modify the active-reading questions embedded in the selection as follows:

- What did people think might happen to Yellowstone because of the fires? (question 1, page 93)
- How are forest fires helpful? (question 4, page 94)

You might also wish to use these alternative questions for discussion:

- How do forests depend on fires?
- How have tourists benefited from the Yellowstone fires?

Here are some suggestions to modify "First Thoughts on Your Reading" on page 95:

- How does the writer want readers to feel after reading the first two paragraphs that describe the fires of 1988? (question 1)
- How do you think people might react to forest fires in the future? (question 3)

READING SKILL: INFERRING CAUSES AND EFFECTS (PAGES 95–97) To help ELL students understand the meaning of *infer*, give this example: The deer ran out of the forest into the clearing, just ahead of the smoke. Ask students to guess what caused the deer to run. Students may suggest that the deer ran because of a forest fire since the example included a detail about smoke. Tell students that they have made an inference. Explain that *to infer* means "to make an educated guess based on information."

You may also want to go over the list of causative verbs on page 96 with ELL students. Pair ELL students with native English speakers and have each pair explain the cause-and-effect relationship in the sentences where the causative verbs appear. Allow each pair to discuss one of their explanations. This gives ELL students an opportunity to practice their speaking skills.

READING FOCUS: CAUSE-AND-EFFECT STRUCTURE (PAGES 97–101) In this section, ELL students may require assistance with the concepts *organizational pattern, composite patterns,* and *causal chain.*

- ELL students might find the graphic organizers in this section especially useful to visualize these concepts. Develop a discussion based on the three organizational patterns on pages 98–99. Point out that each shows a full cause-and-effect relationship. One emphasizes causes. Another focuses on effects. The last focuses on an initial cause, intermediate causes or effects, and a final effect. A composite pattern, as illustrated on page 100, looks at the connections between all the cause-effect relationships using more than one organizational pattern.
- Before ELL students complete the exercise in Your Turn 3 on page 101, give them enough time to re-read the article and ask any necessary clarifying questions. Students can work on the exercise in small groups.

Examining Causes and Effects (continued)

WRITING WORKSHOP:

Writing a Cause-and-Effect Explanation (pages 104–121)

Building Background

PREWRITING (PAGES 104–109) ELL students will benefit from focusing on these tasks as they prepare to write a cause-and-effect explanation:

- Help students to write conditional statements in an "If-Then Log," as suggested on page 104. This syntactic structure shows cause-and-effect relationships clearly and gives students practice with conditionals.

- The practice exercises in the Critical Thinking Mini-Lesson on page 108, "Oversimplification and False Cause and Effect," can help students identify faulty thinking in cause-and-effect explanations. Allow ELL students to justify their answers orally.

- Students can first illustrate the causes and effects in a picture or a series of frames, or students might want to create a graphic organizer. Allow time for students to explain their illustrations or diagrams to a partner or to a small group. This exercise helps ELL students explore and expand vocabulary for their cause-and-effect explanations.

Working with Text Structures

WRITING (PAGES 110–113) These strategies may help ELL students as they write cause-and-effect explanations:

- ELL students may not be familiar with the structure or component parts of a typical cause-and-effect explanation. Review the Framework for a cause-and-effect explanation on page 110 and show students how the parts mentioned in the Framework appear in A Writer's Model on pages 111–112 and A Student's Model on page 113. You may wish to provide some other brief examples of cause-and-effect explanations using student samples you have collected. Have students identify the structure of these additional models.

- Since ELL students are still acquiring writing proficiency in English, you might have them develop a shorter composition.

REVISING (PAGES 114–117) ELL students might find it helpful to concentrate on a few of the items in the Content and Organization Guidelines on page 114. Questions 2, 3, and 5 are important, as they focus on the essential elements of the cause-and-effect essay.

Examining Causes and Effects *(continued)*

Working with Sentence Structures

SECOND READING: STYLE (PAGES 115–117) ELL students may understand infinitives fairly easily because many languages have a base form of the verb. Guide ELL students through the "One Writer's Revisions" on page 116 and ask students to revise one sentence in their essays so that it begins with an infinitive or an infinitive phrase.

Working with Grammar

DANGLING MODIFIERS (PAGE 118) Depending on how much experience they have with sentence construction in their native languages, ELL students may have difficulty recognizing dangling modifiers. Review the examples and practice items in the Grammar Link on page 118 and have students work with proficient English speakers to locate any problems with dangling modifiers in their essays. You may also wish to assign the exercises on pages 626–627 as additional practice.

FOCUS ON VIEWING AND REPRESENTING:

Analyzing the Effects of TV (pages 122–124)

Building Viewing and Representing Skills

If ELL students are not familiar with the current TV shows that depict careers, ask native English speakers in the class to describe these shows. If possible, allow time for ELL students to view clips of TV shows.

To help students prepare for their interviews, have students work in pairs to make a list of questions they can ask people in the careers they are investigating. Allow partners to practice asking the questions.

CHOICES:

(page 125)

Making Curricular Connections/Relating to Personal Experiences

CROSSING THE CURRICULUM: LITERATURE 4. MOTIVATIONS AND CONSEQUENCES (PAGE 125) Modify this activity by allowing ELL students to choose works of fiction written by authors from their native countries.

Analyzing Problems

Chapter Objectives:
- To read a problem-analysis article
- To write an analysis of a problem
- To prepare and deliver an informative speech
- To recognize news genres and analyze news coverage

Key Concepts for English-Language Learners:
Frequent repetition, in a variety of contexts, will aid ELL students' understanding of key ideas in academic discourse. As you work through the chapter, use the following concepts frequently: *purpose, audience, tone, fact, statistic, expert testimony,* and *anecdote.*

PREVIEW: ## Introducing the Chapter (pages 126–127)

Making Cultural Connections
As you introduce the chapter, keep in mind that students from different cultures may have different approaches to solving problems. If the problem is personal, students from some cultures may ask older family members or an important member of the community for advice, while others may seek no advice. In some cultures, open discussion of political or social problems and possible solutions is simply not done, and some ELL students may find it difficult to enter into such discussions. In other cultures, the same holds true regarding the discussion of personal problems. Ask students to share with the class how problem solving would be approached in their cultures.

Building Background/Relating to Personal Experiences
1. To respect the comfort levels of some ELL students, you may want to discuss problem-solution experiences in a more general sense by asking the following questions:

    - When you hear the words *problem* and *solution*, what do you think of?
    - Think about a problem you have heard or read about recently. How did the person or group try to solve the problem? Did the person or group have any help?

2. ELL students may need simple prompts to participate in the discussion about the illustration on page 126. Ask students to discuss the arrows and the direction of the man's arms:

    - Which way do the man's arms point?
    - Which way does the large arrow point?
    - Which way does the small arrow point?
    - What might these details tell viewers about choices?

One way to interpret the picture is that it represents different choices about problems—choices you might analyze before deciding on a solution.

READING WORKSHOP:

Reading a Problem-Analysis Article (pages 128–137)

Building Background/Relating to Personal Experiences

Conduct a survey with your ELL students about cell phones by asking the following questions:

- How many people do you know who own cell phones?
- How many people do you know who use them while driving?
- Have you ever witnessed an accident or near-accident when a driver was using a cell phone?

Working with Academic Language/Building Vocabulary

PREPARING TO READ (PAGE 128) Before ELL students read the problem-analysis article, be sure they understand the terms *generalization, evidence, facts, statistics,* and *anecdotes,* which are introduced on page 128. Make connections to students' activities in the "Introducing the Chapter" section. Write the terms on the board, and encourage students to give examples of each term. Jot down student responses on the board, too. This exercise gives students a chance to work with terminology in context.

READING THE SELECTION (PAGES 129–131) Before reading the selection, present the following vocabulary, which may be unfamiliar to ELL students: *chatting, engrossed, sailed through, broadsided, searing, extricated, dismissed, cues, peripheral, suppressed, pinpoint,* and *impaired.*

You may also wish to present the Vocabulary Mini-lesson, "Context Clues: Definitions and Restatements," on page 136 before students read the article. This will give students a strategy for figuring out the meaning of unfamiliar words as they read the article. Remind students that this strategy can also be very helpful as they read the instructional text in the chapter. For additional context clue strategies, refer students to page 887 of the Quick Reference Handbook.

To guide students through reading this selection, choose from the general strategies for vocabulary and comprehension provided at the beginning of this booklet. In addition, you may want to modify the active-reading questions in the selection as follows:

Analyzing Problems *(continued)*

- The article begins with a real-life tragedy. How do you think this affects readers? (question 1, page 129)
- What statistic does the writer give that suggests cell phones are dangerous? (question 3, page 129)
- How is the use of other electronic gadgets in cars like the use of cell phones? (question 6, page 131)

Another way to approach the active-reading questions is to provide alternative questions for students to discuss, for example:

- What does the writer want you to think about cell phones?
- How does the use of direct quotes affect how you feel about this topic?

READING SKILL: MAKING GENERALIZATIONS (PAGES 132–134) What is clearly a qualifying word to native English speakers may not be obvious to ELL students. Guide ELL students to recognize generalizations. Jot these examples from the article on the board:

- "We're a society on the run, and to save time, we conduct business, chat with friends, make our arrangements—all from the car." (page 129)
- "But a bigger problem is the mental distraction caused by talking on the phone." (page 130)

Prompt students to analyze the basis of each statement and to state whether they think the generalization has enough information. Point out *bigger* as a qualifying word.

READING FOCUS: PROBLEM-SOLUTION STRUCTURE (PAGES 134–135) To give ELL students more practice with problem-solution structure, suggest a current problem in your school, such as large classes or lack of new uniforms for the school band. Students can decide if the issue needs a problem focus or a solution focus by using the charts on page 135.

WRITING WORKSHOP:

Writing a Problem-Analysis Essay (pages 138–157)

Building Background

PREWRITING (PAGES 138–145) ELL students' writing fluency may lag significantly behind their fluency in reading and speaking. Consider the following modifications to help students develop their problem-analysis essays:

- Guide students toward topics that relate to their experiences. Make a list of possible topics using the suggestions at the top of page 139. Take a survey to see which topics might be of interest.

Analyzing Problems (continued)

- Since ELL students are acquiring writing vocabularies, help them focus on a single, well-defined audience for their essays. This focus will enable students to concentrate more easily on details that relate to their audiences.
- Because an interview involves a structured exchange of language, some ELL students might not be as relaxed and receptive as they would be during an informal social conversation. Give a mini-lesson on interviewing using the Teaching Tip on page 141 in the Annotated Teacher's Edition. This activity provides ELL students opportunities to develop their oral language skills and to sharpen their listening skills.
- Have students use two colored highlighters to indicate the problem and solution in their thesis statements.
- Once students have gathered and organized information for their essays, suggest that they present their ideas orally to a small group. Group members can tell speakers if they have enough support for their key points. Group members may also suggest alternate organizational patterns.

Working with Text Structures

WRITING (PAGES 146–149) While the topic in A Writer's Model on pages 147–148 may be familiar to students, they may not be familiar with the structure or component parts of a typical problem-analysis essay. Review the Framework for a problem-analysis essay on page 146. Guide students to key points in A Writer's Model on pages 147–148 and A Student's Model on page 149.

REVISING (PAGES 150–154) It might help to pair ELL students with native English speakers. Establish some principles of peer editing as ELL students conduct the first reading of their drafts. Give the following guidelines or adapt them as needed:

- The writer may read the draft aloud or ask the reader to read silently.
- The reader should focus on each question in the Content and Organization Guidelines on page 150 (or specifically on questions 2, 3, and 4).
- The reader should offer positive comments first, then make suggestions for revisions in constructive ways, such as, "This point needs support. Could you add something?" or "This sounds like an opinion, not a fact. You might want to restate it."

Building Vocabulary

SECOND READING: STYLE (PAGE 151–153) Depending on sentence constructions in their native languages, ELL students may have difficulty with the concept "word wasters." Some languages tend to use more elaborate constructions, so some ELL students might not readily detect this problem in their essays. Here are a few suggestions:

- Review the examples in the Focus on Word Choice on page 152. Have ELL students work with proficient English speakers to locate any problems with "word wasters" in their essays.
- To help students answer question 2 in Analyzing the Revision Process on page 153, review the definitions of *phrase* and *clause*.

Working with Grammar

SENTENCE FRAGMENTS (PAGE 155) ELL students may have difficulty with sentence fragments. ELL students might perceive fragments in oral language as meaningful units because they are enhanced by intonation. Explain the differences between oral and written communication. Then, review the examples and practice items in the Grammar Link on page 155. Remind students that complete sentences must have both a subject and a predicate. Have students work with proficient English speakers to locate any problems with sentence fragments in their essays.

FOCUS ON SPEAKING AND LISTENING:

Giving an Informative Speech (pages 158–161)

Building Speaking and Listening Skills

Since ELL students are already familiar with their problem-analysis essays, you may want them to use that material for their informative speeches. Students may:

- use the Framework on page 146 and develop outlines of their essays to use for notes
- practice giving their speeches to a small group or into a tape recorder

FOCUS ON VIEWING AND REPRESENTING:

Recognizing News Genres (pages 162–164)

Building Viewing and Representing Skills

ELL students may not be familiar with the existing variety of news genres available to viewers in the United States. If possible, plan class time to view videotaped clips or live broadcasts of nightly news programs, newsmagazine shows, and documentaries. Use the questions on page 163 to guide a discussion about each program. Then, ask students what news sources are typically available in their native countries.

Analyzing Problems *(continued)*

CHOICES: | **(page 165)**

Building Speaking and Listening Skills

CAREERS: 1. GIVE A CHECKUP (PAGE 165) Through this activity, ELL students can use oral English language skills in relatively new areas. Here are some suggestions for students:

- Write a list of questions to ask at the interview.
- Create a poster or other graphic display of the information you gather.
- Use the poster as a visual aid for your oral report.
- Make comparisons to the same profession in your native country.

Analyzing a Short Story

Chapter Objectives:
- To read a literary analysis
- To write a literary analysis
- To critique a film
- To present an oral interpretation

Key Concepts for English-Language Learners:
Use the following key concepts frequently, and in a variety of contexts, to support ELL students' understanding of important ideas: *analysis, conclusions, inference,* and *literary elements.*

PREVIEW: Introducing the Chapter (pages 166–167)

Making Cultural Connections
As you introduce the chapter, keep in mind that analyses of literary elements in short stories may not be as prevalent in other cultures. Throughout the chapter, encourage students to refer to short stories they have read in their native languages. You may wish to have students give brief descriptions of some of their favorite stories. Discuss why stories are popular the world over. What is their appeal?

Relating to Personal Experiences
To introduce the chapter, encourage ELL students to discuss things they already know how to analyze. Use prompts such as the following:

- What's in your favorite dish? Why do you enjoy it so much?
- How do you make a play in a sport, such as hockey, basketball, or lacrosse?
- Think about a short story you have read. Was the story funny or sad? Was there much action? Were the characters like real people?

Building Background
1. Before viewing the illustration on page 166, go over the concept *analysis.* Then, ask ELL students to look at the illustration and identify the separate parts. Finally, have students explain how the parts work together.

2. Have ELL students do the alternative Your Turn 1 activity that is suggested on page 167 in the Annotated Teacher's Edition. Familiarity with a recent movie may help ELL students focus directly on the points for analysis. The activity can help you informally assess ELL students' working understanding of literary elements.

Analyzing a Short Story (continued)

READING WORKSHOP:

Reading a Literary Analysis (pages 168–177)

Building Background

Some ELL students may not be familiar with Charles Dickens and *A Christmas Carol.* Provide a synopsis of the plot, setting, and characters. Students will especially need to understand the background of the time in which the novel is set. You may also wish to show some clips from one of the movie versions.

Since some ELL students may not be familiar with literary analysis as a writing form, have a brief discussion in which you explain what a literary analysis is, where it is usually found, and what its purpose is. You may also wish to provide examples from the literary review section of school, local, or national newspapers or magazines to familiarize students with analyses. You may also ask students to find examples on their own.

Working with Academic Language/Building Vocabulary

PREPARING TO READ (PAGE 168) Before you present the literary analysis on pages 169–171, be sure students understand the meaning of the following terms introduced on page 168: *conclusions, inference, plot, setting, character, point of view, theme,* and *language.*

READING THE SELECTION (PAGES 169–171) Before reading the selection, present the following vocabulary, which may be unfamiliar to ELL students: *tale, refrain, miserliness, shunning, insipid, abiding, grizzled, detractors, malady,* and *benediction.*

To provide ELL students with a strategy for figuring out the meanings of unfamiliar words, you may want to present the Vocabulary Mini-lesson, "Using Roots," on page 176. Remind ELL students to use this strategy as they read the selection as well as the instructional text in the chapter.

To guide students through the literary analysis, select from the general strategies provided at the beginning of this booklet. You may wish to read aloud, one at a time, the questions embedded in the selection, and then read the section of the analysis to which it applies. In addition, you may wish to modify the active-reading questions embedded in the selection, for example:

- How does the author describe Dickens's writing? (question 1, page 169)
- What words in this paragraph describe the character of Ebenezer Scrooge? (question 2, page 170)

- Why did Dickens want to stay in contact with his child-hood? (question 4, page 170)
- According to Dickens, why didn't Scrooge interact with Tiny Tim? (question 5, page 171)

In addition, ELL students should recognize how Irving uses quotations from *A Christmas Carol* throughout his analysis to support the points he makes. Tell students to look for words in quotation marks to identify these story excerpts.

READING SKILL: DRAWING CONCLUSIONS (PAGES 172–173) Consider the following activities to help ELL students understand the concept *drawing conclusions:*

- To introduce ELL students to the concept *drawing conclusions,* read the following situations out loud. Ask students to figure out what information they can infer.

    1. Your friend puts on a raincoat and gets an umbrella before going out. (It is raining)

    2. You study hard for a test. When you get the test paper, you know most of the answers. (You will probably get a good grade.)

    3. The school bus picks you up at 7:30 every morning. One morning, you sleep until 7:15. By the time you get to the bus stop it is 7:35. (You have probably missed the bus.)

- Stress to ELL students that their conclusions about a literary work, based on content and their knowledge and experiences, can be just as valid as anyone else's conclusion. If necessary, work together through number 1 in Your Turn 2 on page 173 to give students more confidence with this concept before they complete the exercise.

READING FOCUS: LITERARY ELEMENTS (PAGES 173–175) Make ELL students aware that not every literary analysis discusses all the literary elements in depth. Writers usually choose one or more elements, depending on the focus of their analyses. For practice in analyzing literary elements, choose one element, such as character. Then, use a familiar short story to show how a writer can analyze the element according to the definition listed on the chart on page 174. You may want to think of questions students can ask themselves to analyze the element. For example, when analyzing a character, students can ask what a character looks like, how he or she acts, and how other characters feel about him or her.

Analyzing a Short Story (continued)

WRITING WORKSHOP:

Writing a Literary Analysis (pages 178–197)

Building Background

PREWRITING (PAGES 178–183) ELL students may have a greater facility with reading and speaking English text than they do with writing English text. Consider the following modifications to help students develop their literary analyses of a short story:

- Encourage students to use short stories that are at their English language reading levels. You might also suggest that ELL students read short stories written in their native languages, and for which an English translation is available.
- After students answer the questions in the chart on pages 179–180, they can highlight the most in-depth information. This might help them choose a focus and develop a thesis.
- To help students understand *elaboration* (page 183), suggest that they ask this question about each key point: What does the key point suggest about the deeper meaning of the story?

Working with Text Structures

WRITING (PAGES 184–187) Consider some of these approaches to help ELL students have a satisfying writing experience:

- Allow time for students to read "A Man Called Horse" by Dorothy M. Johnson before they read the analysis on pages 185–186. This will help them understand the selection better and apply that understanding to the literary analyses they write.
- ELL students may not be familiar with the Framework described on page 184. Show students how A Writer's Model on pages 185–186 and A Student's Model on page 187 reflect the Framework.
- Since ELL students are still acquiring writing proficiency in English, you might suggest that they limit their analyses to examining only one literary element.

REVISING (PAGES 188–192) ELL students may find it more manageable to concentrate on fewer items in the Content and Organization Guidelines on page 188. Questions 3, 4, and 5 focus on the essential elements of a literary analysis.

Working with Grammar

USING QUOTATION MARKS IN A LITERARY ANALYSIS (PAGE 193)
Depending on how much experience they have with quotation marks, ELL students may have difficulty using them in a literary analysis. Keep in mind that the conventions for punctuating quotations differ among languages. For example, when quotation marks are used in Spanish, periods and commas are

always placed outside the closing quotation marks. However, it is more common to use long dashes to set off quotations in Spanish. Review the examples and practice items in the Grammar Link on page 193 and have students work with proficient English speakers to locate any problems with quotation marks in their analyses.

FOCUS ON VIEWING AND REPRESENTING:

Critiquing a Film (pages 198–202)

Building Viewing and Representing Skills

ELL students may benefit from viewing the film more than once. Suggest that they form small groups in which each student chooses one element of the film to focus on for a group report. Tell students to use the elements in the charts on pages 199–200. However, allow students to add elements they feel are appropriate for the film they are critiquing.

FOCUS ON SPEAKING AND LISTENING:

Presenting an Oral Interpretation (pages 203–204)

Building Speaking and Listening Skills

ELL students may feel more comfortable participating in a group oral interpretation. Allow time for the students to practice their presentations. You may also want to refer students to page 905 in the Quick Reference Handbook for more tips on presenting an oral interpretation.

CHOICES:

(page 205)

Relating to Personal Experiences

VIEWING AND REPRESENTING: 4. ILLUSTRATE A CHILDREN'S BOOK (PAGE 205)
Suggest that ELL students choose a popular children's book from their native countries, present a synopsis to the class, and draw an illustration or create a collage or poster that represents the theme of the story.

Chapter Objectives:
- To read a research article
- To write a research paper
- To evaluate Web sites

Key Concepts for English-Language Learners:
ELL students often require frequent repetition, in a variety of contexts, in order to understand key ideas in academic discourse. As you work through the chapter, use the following key concepts frequently: *research, investigation, paraphrase, primary source, secondary source,* and *citing sources.*

PREVIEW: ## Introducing the Chapter (pages 206–207)

Relating to Personal Experience
To introduce the chapter, provide opportunities for ELL students to share their own knowledge of research and investigation. Use one of the following activities to explore research:

- When you hear the words *research* and *investigation,* what do you think of?
- Have ELL students think about questions for which they needed information this week. For example, students may say that they needed to know the price of something, the location of something, or directions to get somewhere or do something. Encourage students to explain how they tried to find the answers.
- Challenge students to make a collage representing the kinds of information they frequently access or would like to access.

Building Background
Put ELL students into small groups to formulate questions that can prompt investigation. Suggest categories such as *people, places, inventions,* and so on. Allow students to share their questions and then, discuss places where students may find answers. This discussion will lay the groundwork for research concepts.

Making Cultural Connections
ELL students may have varied experiences with finding and sharing information. Some students may feel that class assignments should be done alone; others may be comfortable with collaboration. Your awareness of and sensitivity to students' different experiences and comfort levels with sharing information will help you address their concerns or anxieties as you work through this chapter. If it seems right for your class, open a discussion about collaboration, the free access of most

information in the United States, and ELL students' experiences with these issues elsewhere.

READING WORKSHOP:

Reading a Research Article (pages 208–217)

Building Background

Begin a discussion with ELL students about articles they have read. Were the articles in magazines, academic journals, or on internet sites? Guide the discussion with the following prompts and any others you wish to add:

- What were the purposes of the articles you read?
- What kinds of information have you learned from them?
- What was the tone of articles you read?

Working with Academic Language/Building Vocabulary

PREPARING TO READ (PAGE 208) Before you present the article on pages 209–212, be sure that ELL students understand the terms *primary source* and *secondary source*. Give these examples of primary and secondary sources in addition to those cited on page 208:

- Primary sources: autobiographies, interviews, historical documents, original research
- Secondary sources: books and articles based on information from primary sources, summary reports, encyclopedias

Remind students that secondary sources can be as useful as primary sources and are often more readily available.

READING THE SELECTION (PAGES 209–212) To guide students through reading this selection, choose from the general strategies for vocabulary and comprehension provided at the beginning of this booklet.

Before reading the selection on pages 209–212, present unfamiliar vocabulary to ELL students. Be sure students understand the meanings of the following words in the article: *flustered, exotic, evoke, subliminal, hovering, assumption, unscrupulous, enigmatic, outmoded, baby boomers, narcissism, uptightness,* and *bleak.*

You may also wish to present the Vocabulary Mini-lesson, "Specialized and Technical Terms," on page 216. Remind ELL students to use this strategy as they read the selection as well as the instructional text in the chapter.

Use the active-reading questions embedded in the selection to do a guided reading. Ask one question at a time, and have students read surrounding text for the answer. You could also modify some of the active-reading questions, for example:

- What words does the writer use to let you know his opinion of the new Australian money? (question 6, page 210)
- What did the author say about the people shown on bills? (question 7, page 211)
- What experience do the people in international travel agencies have with various currencies? (question 9, page 211)

You may also want to use these additional or alternative questions for students to discuss:

- How would you describe the tone of this article?
- What does the writer want you to learn about money?
- Is this a believable article? Why or why not?

READING SKILL: PARAPHRASING (PAGES 213–214) Paraphrasing can be daunting to ELL students who do not have adequate vocabularies or expressive fluency. Focus on paraphrasing as a tool for checking understanding. Present the Thinking It Through, "Paraphrasing a Passage," and Your Turn 2 on page 214 as a guided group activity. To help ELL students gather their thoughts, you might encourage them to paraphrase in their native languages before paraphrasing in English.

READING FOCUS: PRIMARY AND SECONDARY SOURCES (PAGES 214–215) In this section, ELL students will require assistance with the terms *primary source, secondary source, formal research*, and *informal research*. Bring in examples of primary and secondary sources and formal and informal research articles. Discuss with students how they differ.

WRITING WORKSHOP: Writing a Research Paper (pages 218–246)

Building Background/Relating to Personal Experience
PREWRITING (PAGES 218–231) ELL students may not have much experience developing research topics. Consider the following modifications to help students develop their papers:

- Guide students toward topics that interest them or relate to their own experiences.
- As students think about purpose and audience, remind them that readers in the United States may be especially interested in topics about ELL students' native countries, even if ELL students consider those topics ordinary.

- Sometimes, ELL students will not be able to formulate questions until they have read a bit about the topic. This process often turns up points that spark students' interest and motivates them to research.

- Make sure that a school librarian has given ELL students an orientation to research tools in the library. For example, students will need to know how to use the card catalog and special resource indexes. They may also need to be shown how to locate reliable on-line sources.

- ELL students may not be familiar with many of the sources of information available to them. You may wish to pair ELL students with fluent English speakers to explore examples of the sources listed in the chart on pages 222–223.

- If you are using the MLA format, provide ELL students with samples of source cards for different kinds of sources. Make sure students use the information in "Guidelines for Recording Source Information" on pages 224–225. These handy samples will help students remember how to record complete source information.

- Suggest other methods of organizing the research materials students gather, such as file folders or color-coded cards.

- Have students use a large surface to arrange their materials in whatever kind of order works best for them. Ask students to discuss their organization with a native English speaker and get some feedback on whether it is logical.

Working with Text Structures

WRITING (PAGES 232–239) Use some of the following tips to guide ELL students as they write their research papers:

- Review the Framework for a research paper on page 232 and show students how the parts described in the Framework appear in A Writer's Model on pages 233–235 and A Student's Model on page 236.

- If ELL students have difficulty writing a good introduction, suggest that they write the body of their papers first, then come back to the introduction.

- To help ELL students avoid plagiarism, review the concept of *paraphrasing* on pages 213–214. In addition, make sure students use the "Guidelines for Giving Credit Within a Paper" on pages 237–238.

REVISING (PAGES 240–243) ELL students may find it helpful to concentrate on items 2, 3, and 4 in the Content and Organization Guidelines on page 240.

- You may also suggest to ELL students who are drafting their papers on computers to make a duplicate of their original drafts. That way they can revise the duplicate copy and look back at the original during the revising process.

Working with Sentence Structures

SECOND READING: STYLE (PAGES 241–243) For ELL students acquiring English writing skills, varying sentence length may be difficult. Also, ELL students' writing vocabularies and understanding of sentence structure may be somewhat limited. Use sentences from students' papers, and work with the group to develop models for varying sentence length. Then, have partners work together and choose two or three sentences in their articles to revise according to the models.

Working with Grammar

CORRECTING MISPLACED MODIFIERS (PAGE 244) Placement of modifiers can be different in ELL students' native languages than it is in English. Review the examples and practice items in the Grammar Link on page 244 and have students work with proficient English speakers to identify and resolve any problems with misplaced modifiers in their papers. For additional explanation and practice, refer students to pages 627–631.

FOCUS ON VIEWING AND REPRESENTING:

Evaluating Web Sites (pages 247–248)

Building Viewing and Representing Skills

To help ELL students evaluate Web sites, they can make charts with the characteristics of a valid site as presented in the chart on page 248. Students can view several sites and record relevant information in an easily accessible format.

Web site	Objective	Reliable	Complete	Clear	Current	Accurate

CHOICES:

(page 249)

Making Cultural Connections/Relating to Personal Experiences

LITERATURE: 2. YOUR VERY OWN BOOK CLUB (PAGE 249) ELL students might enjoy introducing books from their native countries to classmates. Encourage ELL students to find an English translation of the book and information about the author. Cultural ideas and visions can be exchanged through such a discussion.

Sharing Research Results *(continued)*

CROSSING THE CURRICULUM: THE ARTS: 3. YOUR ART FORM (PAGE 249)
ELL students may enjoy presenting their chosen art forms in addition to the writing. Set aside time for students to bring in music recordings or pictures of paintings or sculptures. Some students may want to show their own art or to perform. Encourage ELL students to acquaint classmates with forms of art from their native cultures.

Persuading Others

Chapter Objectives:
- to read a persuasive newspaper article
- to write a persuasive essay
- to analyze editorial cartoons
- to give a persuasive speech

Key Concepts for English-Language Learners:

ELL students often require frequent repetition, in a variety of contexts, in order to understand key ideas in academic discourse. As you work through the chapter, use the following key concepts frequently: *persuasion, fact, opinion, opinion statement, logical appeal, reasons, evidence, emotional appeal, connotative words,* and *anecdote.*

PREVIEW: ## Introducing the Chapter (pages 250–251)

Relating to Personal Experience

1. To introduce the chapter, provide opportunities for ELL students to share their own experiences and knowledge of persuasion. Use one of the following prompts to explore the concept:

   - Tell about a time when someone persuaded you to do something. What finally changed your mind?
   - When you hear the term *persuasion*, what do you think about?
   - What are some different ways that people persuade others to agree with them?

2. For an oral language development activity that addresses persuasion, ask students to role play persuasive situations. Groups of three or four students can perform role-plays based on the following scenarios:

   - Persuade your parents to allow you to take a summer job.
   - Persuade a business owner to hire you for a summer job.
   - Persuade your friends to go on a three-mile walk to benefit the homeless.

After groups perform their role-plays, ask them to discuss what they did to be persuasive. Ask the class to critique whether the performers were persuasive. This discussion will lay the groundwork for the chapter.

Persuading Others *(continued)*

Building Background

ELL students may need help understanding the advertisement on page 250. On the board, write the words *calcium* and *recommended*. Go over the words before discussing the ad. Ask students what they know about calcium. Elicit that calcium is important for the development of strong bones and teeth. If necessary, explain that milk is an important source of calcium, so three glasses a day are *recommended,* or suggested, in order to stay healthy. Make sure that students are familiar with Cal Ripken, Jr.

Have students work in small groups to discuss the ad. Pair ELL students with students who are proficient or native English speakers. Have students ask each other the following questions:

- Why does Cal Ripken drink milk?
- Why does he say his name might as well be Calcium Ripken, Jr.?
- Why does the ad show Ripken with a milk mustache?
- What does the ad want us to do?
- Does the ad convince you? Why or why not?

As you discuss the ad, emphasize the importance of word choice. Guide ELL students to understand that different words would have different effects on the readers. Point out that this ad is one of a series in which celebrities wear milk mustaches.

Making Cultural Connections

As you introduce the chapter, keep in mind that the concepts *persuasion* and *opinion* may be expressed differently in other cultures. For example, ELL students might have less experience with persuasive techniques because of a lack of exposure to advertisements in electronic or print media. Ask ELL students to describe the kinds of ads familiar in their native cultures and to compare those ads with ones typically found in the United States.

READING WORKSHOP: ## Reading a Persuasive Newspaper Article (pages 252–262)

Building Background

Some ELL students may not be familiar with the persuasive newspaper article as a journalistic form. Have a brief discussion in which you help students understand what persuasive newspaper articles are, who writes them, what their purposes are, and where they are found. Provide examples from local and national newspapers for students to see differences in format and appearance. You may also wish to have students bring in examples of their own.

To prepare students for the content of the article, ask volunteers to describe their impressions of airport, train, or bus waiting areas. Guide students to describe sights, sounds, crowds, and confusion that they may have experienced in such places.

Working with Academic Language/Building Vocabulary

PREPARING TO READ (PAGE 252) Before you present the persuasive newspaper article on pages 253–254, be sure that ELL students understand the terms *fact, opinion, opinion statements, reasons, evidence,* and *emotional appeals,* which are introduced on page 252. Help students make a connection to their activities in the "Introducing the Chapter" section: Ask them to give examples of facts, opinions, and emotional appeals used in their role-plays. Make sure that students understand the difference between facts, which can be proved, and opinions, which cannot be proved. This discussion can help students link their experiences to the academic language specific to persuasion.

READING THE SELECTION (PAGES 253–254) Before reading the selection, present unfamiliar vocabulary to students. Be sure students understand the meanings of the following words used in the persuasive newspaper article on pages 253–254: *force-fed, meditative, distractions, widespread, relentlessly, proliferating,* and *creeping.* Go over the words and keep them on the board for reference. Add new words at any time during the lesson.

You may also wish to present the Vocabulary Mini-Lesson, "Understanding Connotations and Denotations," on page 261 before students read the persuasive article. The semantics may be particularly difficult for ELL students to grasp as they are acquiring a basic vocabulary. Many students still need to attend to particular words in a variety of contexts before comprehending shades of meaning. You might also suggest that ELL students consult a bilingual dictionary or an English-language thesaurus to recognize shades of meaning.

To guide students through reading the article, select from the general strategies provided at the beginning of this booklet. In addition, you may wish to modify the active-reading questions embedded in the selection, for example:

- What facts does the author provide about TV in public places? (question 2, page 253)

Persuading Others (continued) PAGES 250-293

- What effects do the words *captive, strenuous,* and *creeping* have on the reader? (question 3, page 254)
- What sentence in this paragraph tells you how the author feels about TV in public places? (question 5, page 254)

Another way to approach the active-reading questions is to provide alternative questions for students to discuss, for example:

- How does the author feel about televisions in public?
- What would the author like to see changed?
- Do you agree with the author? Why or why not?

You may also wish to modify "First Thoughts on Your Reading" on page 255 in this way:

- Where did the author put his opinion statement? Why? (question 1)
- Which words and images are the strongest? (question 2)
- How does the author make you feel about televisions in public places? (question 3)

READING SKILL: DISTINGUISHING FACTS FROM OPINION (PAGES 255–257)
Discuss Thinking It Through on page 256 with students. Call their attention to semantic markers that often signal opinion: indefinite terms such as *few* or *many*; generalization clue words such as *all, every, always, never*; opinion clue words such as *should* and *must*; and words that signal value such as *best* and *worst*. Have students find examples in "Force-Fed Television."

Ask ELL students to work in pairs or small groups as they complete Your Turn 2 on page 257. Encourage them to identify semantic markers in the opinion statements.

READING FOCUS: ELEMENTS OF PERSUASION (PAGES 257–260) In this section, ELL students will benefit from assistance with the concepts *logical appeals, emotional appeals, connotative words,* and *anecdotes.* Consider the following suggestions:

- To help clarify the difference between logical and emotional appeals, present a position statement to the class such as: *Television newscasters should simply present the news without adding personal commentary.* Divide the class into small groups; have each group develop one of the particular types of appeal and share it with the class.
- Guide students to find examples of each of the above concepts in the reading selection.
- Ask students if they can cite examples of these persuasive elements in some of the articles they have brought to class.

Persuading Others (continued)

WRITING WORKSHOP:

Writing a Persuasive Essay (pages 263–283)

Building Background/Relating to Personal Experiences

PREWRITING (PAGES 263–271) Consider the following modifications to help students develop a persuasive essay:

- Guide students in choosing a topic that is important to them and that relates to their experiences. For example, ELL students may want to write about the importance of being bilingual, or they could write about preserving a culture's language and traditions.
- Guide ELL students to identify their audiences. Help them consider social and cultural variables that would affect audience responses, such as customs, geographical location, education, age, and interests.

Working with Text Structures

WRITING (PAGES 272–275) Consider some of these approaches to help ELL students have a satisfying experience writing a persuasive essay:

- ELL students might not be familiar with the structure or components of a typical persuasive essay: attention-grabbing opener, background information, opinion statement, supporting reasons, evidence, thesis restatement, and a call to action. Review the Framework for writing a persuasive essay on page 272 and show students how the parts mentioned in the Framework appear in A Writer's Model on pages 273–274 and A Student's Model on page 275. You may also wish to provide some other brief examples of student writing. Have students identify the reasons and evidence in these examples.
- ELL students are still developing basic writing skills in English. Consider assigning a streamlined three-paragraph essay with the following structure:

    Introduction (first paragraph): thesis statement

    Body (second paragraph): one reason with supporting evidence

    Conclusion (third): restatement of the thesis and a call to action

    Encourage students to include graphics such as charts, graphs, captioned illustrations, or photos to convey some of their information.

REVISING (PAGES 276–279) ELL students may find it helpful to concentrate on two or three items in the Content and Organization Guidelines on page 276. Questions 2, 3, and 5 will be especially helpful to them, as these questions focus on the essential elements of a persuasive essay.

Working with Sentence Structures

SECOND READING: STYLE (PAGES 277–279) Some ELL students will naturally fall into using the passive voice initially because they perceive parallels in the structures of their native languages, particularly in languages making extensive use of reflexive verbs. As students become more comfortable writing in English, this preference for the passive voice should fade. Meanwhile, you might wish to bring students to a more immediate awareness of the problem by providing mini-lessons on active and passive voice. Pages 601–605 also contain clear explanations and provide exercises.

Working with Grammar

DOUBLE NEGATIVES (PAGE 280) Depending on particular structures in their native languages, some ELL students will not understand why double negatives should be avoided. To help ELL students recognize double negatives, give them extra practice with negative words. Review the examples and practice items in the Grammar Link on page 280, and have students work with native speakers to identify any problems with double negatives in their papers. You may also wish to direct students to pages 656–657 for more practice identifying and eliminating double negatives.

FOCUS ON VIEWING AND REPRESENTING:

Analyzing Editorial Cartoons (pages 284–287)

Building Viewing and Representing Skills

ELL students may not have enough experience with the culture of the United States to recognize the issues addressed in the cartoons. You may wish to modify the Your Turn activity by having students work in small groups with native English speakers to identify those issues. Once ELL students identify and understand the issues, the remaining questions can be answered independently.

FOCUS ON SPEAKING AND LISTENING:

Giving a Persuasive Speech (pages 288–292)

Building Speaking and Listening Skills

Making a speech in front of an audience can be especially intimidating for ELL students who may worry about their pronunciation and expression. To aid ELL students with this part of the chapter, use the following activities and approaches:

- Encourage ELL students to tape record their speeches. As they replay the speech, they can identify and eliminate problem areas.

- Allow ELL students to practice and present their speeches to small groups of students rather than to the whole class. As they gain confidence with their English skills, ELL students will soon feel more comfortable about speaking to larger groups.

CHOICES:

(page 293)

Making Cultural Connections/Building on Personal Strengths

LITERATURE: 2. POETICALLY PERSUASIVE (PAGE 293) This activity can be a confidence-builder for ELL students. Modify the activity by suggesting that ELL students write a poem or song in their native languages. If they wish, they can teach the words to English-speaking students, explain the meaning, and help with pronunciation. Giving ELL students opportunities to read aloud in their first language validates the importance of their language and increases their confidence by allowing them to be the language expert in the activity. The two-way learning experience also builds a sense of community and friendship among classmates.

Using Persuasion in Advertising

Chapter Objectives:
- To read a persuasive brochure
- To create a persuasive brochure
- To create a documentary on print advertising

Key Concepts for English-Language Learners:
ELL students will benefit from frequent repetition of key concepts in a variety of contexts. As you work through the chapter, use the following key concepts frequently: *persuasive techniques, persuasive visual elements, primary idea, slogan,* and *call to action.*

PREVIEW:

Introducing the Chapter (pages 294–295)

Relating to Personal Experience

1. To introduce the chapter, provide opportunities for ELL students to share their own experiences and knowledge of persuasion in advertising. Use one of the following prompts to help students make personal connections with the topic:

   - Do you ever pick up brochures when you visit museums, historical buildings, or tourist areas? Do you ever pick up brochures from bus or train stations, airports, or other public places? Why or why not?
   - What kinds of information do you expect to find in brochures?
   - Describe a persuasive brochure that you have seen.

2. For a hands-on activity, distribute examples of different types of brochures. For comparison purposes, you may include informational as well as advertising brochures. Ask groups of three or four students to categorize the brochures, and check to see whether they can pick out the brochures that use persuasive techniques. Invite students to critique the effectiveness of the advertising brochures by asking the following questions:

   - Would you pick up this brochure from a rack full of brochures? Why or why not?
   - What attracts your eye when you look at several different brochures?
   - What seems to be the purpose of each brochure?

This discussion lays the groundwork for the concept of using persuasion in advertising.

Using Persuasion in Advertising *(continued)*

Building Background

Explain to ELL students that the chapter opener illustration on page 294 represents the kinds of messages and presentation styles that advertisers use to grab attention. Some students may not understand the meaning of "Nothing Down!" Explain that this means a buyer can purchase a product on credit, without making an immediate cash payment.

Pair ELL students with native English speakers. Have students respond to the following questions about the illustration on page 294:

- What do you notice about the type in the advertisements?
- What effect is created by the use of exclamation points?
- Is color important? Explain.

As students discuss the illustration, emphasize the importance of the combined elements to attract the viewer's or reader's attention.

Making Cultural Connections

ELL students may not have the shared cultural knowledge on which some advertisements base their appeal. Advertisements that refer to historical events or popular culture, or that use humor or celebrity appeal may require special explanation. Ask ELL students to share with the class how some of the sample brochures they have discussed would be received and interpreted in their native cultures. Throughout the chapter activities, look for opportunities to pair ELL students with English-proficient students as a way of building cooperation, appreciation, and understanding.

READING WORKSHOP:

Reading a Persuasive Brochure (pages 296–305)

Building Background/Making Cultural Connections

Have a brief discussion to help ELL students understand what persuasive brochures are, who writes them, what their purposes are, and where they are found. You may wish to make sample brochures available, and encourage students to bring some examples to class as well. Discuss where the brochures were located, what the purpose of each brochure seems to be, and whether or not it is persuasive. Compare and discuss the formats and appearances of different brochures.

Using Persuasion in Advertising *(continued)*   PAGES 294-337

Some ELL students may not be familiar with the topics covered in the reading selection—the bison and the prairie. If necessary, explain what bison are. Review information about the prairie as an ecosystem, and discuss how the prairie has changed since settlers first arrived.

Play the song "Home on the Range" for students. Briefly discuss its theme. Explain that the song is referenced in the brochure because the writer probably counted on its emotional appeal.

Working with Academic Language/Building Vocabulary

PREPARING TO READ (PAGE 296) Before you present the persuasive brochure on pages 297–299, be sure that ELL students understand the terms or phrases *persuasive techniques, logical and emotional appeals, persuasive visual elements, columns, graphics, headings,* and *colors,* which are introduced on page 296. Help students make a connection to the brochures they examined in the "Introducing the Chapter" section: Ask them to give examples of logical and emotional appeals that they noticed in the brochures. What visual elements attracted their attention? This discussion will help students link their previous experiences with persuasive brochures to the reading selection.

Before reading the selection, present unfamiliar vocabulary to students. Be sure students understand the meanings of the following words used in the persuasive brochure on pages 297–299: *restoring, preserving, contribution,* and *legacy.*

To provide ELL students with a strategy for figuring out unfamiliar words, you may also wish to present the Vocabulary Mini-Lesson, "Synonym and Antonym Context Clues," on page 304 before students read the persuasive brochure. Remind students that they can also use this strategy as they read the instructional text in the chapter

READING THE SELECTION (PAGES 297–299) To guide students through reading the brochure, select from the general strategies provided at the beginning of this booklet. In addition, you may wish to modify some of the active-reading questions embedded in the selection, for example:

- Note: Most ELL students will not be able to respond unless they are familiar with the traditional song. If you haven't played the song as part of Building Background, simply have a peer explain the reference. (question 1, page 298)
- What is the message of this brochure? How do the photographs help to get it across? (question 2, page 298)

Using Persuasion in Advertising *(continued)* PAGES 294-337

- What does the Nature Conservancy want you to do? (question 3, page 298)

Another way to approach the active-reading questions is to provide alternative questions for students to discuss, for example:

- Do the headlines on page 297 make you curious and interested in reading more? Explain.
- What is the message of the brochure?
- What does the brochure want the reader to do?
- Why does the brochure include photographs and descriptions of bison?
- What did you learn from the brochure that you didn't know before?

You may also wish to modify "First Thoughts on Your Reading," on page 300 in this way:

- What did you notice first in the brochure? (question 1)
- How did you feel about the different bison as you read their descriptions? (question 2)

READING SKILL: IDENTIFYING PERSUASIVE TECHNIQUES (PAGES 300–302)
The range of ELL students' English vocabularies will affect their ability to recognize bandwagon, transfer, testimonial, and glittering generalities, and to understand their persuasive aspects. Do a mini-lesson on connotation using the examples of persuasive vocabulary presented on pages 300–301. You may also wish to help students search other brochures or magazines and newspaper ads for examples of persuasive techniques.

READING FOCUS: ANALYZING PERSUASIVE VISUAL ELEMENTS (PAGE 303)
Have a sampling of brochures available for reference in addition to the reading selection. Read aloud the chart of "Persuasive Visual Elements" on page 303. Stop after reading each bulleted item and invite students to point out examples of the visual element in the brochures. Then, have students discuss whether that element is used effectively in the brochures.

WRITING WORKSHOP: ## Creating a Persuasive Brochure (pages 306–328)

Building Background/Relating to Personal Experiences
PREWRITING (PAGES 306–315) ELL students may have greater facility speaking in English than writing in English. Consider the following modifications to help students develop a persuasive brochure:

- Encourage ELL students to use the steps in Thinking It Through on page 308 to analyze audience. Partners might want to brainstorm Step 3 together.

Using Persuasion in Advertising *(continued)*   **PAGES 294-337**

- Decide ahead how you wish to address the issue of informal language such as contractions and sentence fragments, both of which often appear in brochures and other advertising materials. You may wish to use the second tip on page 308 as a starting point.

Working with Text Structures

WRITING (PAGES 316–320) Consider some of these approaches to help ELL students have a satisfying writing experience:

- Guide ELL students through the Framework for a persuasive brochure on pages 316–318 by reading aloud each bulleted item and asking students to locate the element in A Writer's Model.
- You may also wish to help students search other brochures or magazines and newspaper ads for examples of persuasive wording. Point out similarities in organization and differences in tone and style.

REVISING (PAGES 321–324) Pair ELL students with students who are proficient native English speakers. ELL students may find it helpful to concentrate on two or three items in the Content and Organization Guidelines on page 321. Questions 2, 4, 5, and 6 will be especially helpful to them, as these questions focus on the essential elements of a persuasive brochure.

Building Vocabulary

SECOND READING: STYLE (PAGES 322–323) Since ELL students are still acquiring a basic English vocabulary, it will be difficult for them to identify clichés. Eliminating clichés may be a challenging concept, as many appear fresh and creative to ELL students. Students may profit from working with native English speakers to identify trite expressions in their brochures and to find fresher ways of conveying the same idea. Have partners work together and come up with original phrasing.

Working with Grammar

CONSISTENT VERB TENSES (PAGE 325) Since many languages other than English do not change verb form to show time, ELL students may have difficulty with consistent verb tenses. Review the examples and practice items in the Grammar Link on page 325, and have students work with native English speakers to identify any problems with inconsistent tenses in their brochures. You may also wish to direct students to the explanations and practice of this concept on pages 597–599.

Using Persuasion in Advertising *(continued)*

FOCUS ON VIEWING AND REPRESENTING:

Creating a Documentary on Print Advertising (pages 329–336)

Building Viewing and Representing Skills

The task of producing a documentary can be overwhelming for ELL students who may not be familiar with the technology. To aid ELL students with this part of the chapter, use the following activities and approaches:

- Bring to class a variety of advertisements from different media to spark students' ideas.
- Locate some documentaries in your school's library and play some clips. Discuss the videos with students, focusing on the organization and elements of the presentation, such as background music.
- Have students work in small groups. Each student can choose a specific "job," such as sound manager, script writer, or camera operator. Guide ELL students to choose a role that is challenging but not overwhelming. Each group member will participate in editing and reviewing the script, so ELL students may enjoy a valuable language experience without having the full responsibility of producing a script.
- Interviews help ELL students develop the ability to formulate questions and to interpret answers. Encourage ELL students to conduct interviews as their contribution to the documentary. Help them plan the questions, anticipate responses, and prepare follow-up questions.

CHOICES:

(page 337)

Making Cultural Connections

MEDIA AND TECHNOLOGY: 4. APPLES *vs.* ORANGES (PAGE 337) ELL students may especially enjoy this activity. You may wish to modify the activity by having students locate advertisements for the same product, or for similar products, both in English and in their native languages. Community newspapers or ethnically oriented newspapers and magazines are sources for such ads. Have students collect examples and share their findings with a small group.